LITTLE GREEN

Growing Up During the Chinese Cultural Revolution

Chun Yu

SCHOLASTIC INC.

ISBN 978-0-545-84727-8

Text and photographs copyright © 2005 by Chun Yu.
Calligraphy copyright © 2005 by Lian Yu. All rights reserved.
Published by Scholastic Inc., 557 Broadway, New York, NY 10012, by arrangement with Paula Wiseman Books, an imprint of Simon & Schuster Children's Publishing Division.
SCHOLASTIC and associated logos are trademarks and/or registered trademarks of Scholastic Inc.

12 11 10 9 8 7 6 5 4 3 2 1   15 16 17 18 19 20/0

Printed in the U.S.A.   40

First Scholastic printing, March 2015

Book design by Mark Siegel
The text for this book is set in Mrs. Eaves.

LITTLE GREEN

For Mama and Baba, who gave me this gift of life.
For Nainai, who brought me up.
For Gege and Sansan, who have shared this life with me.

FAMILY TREE

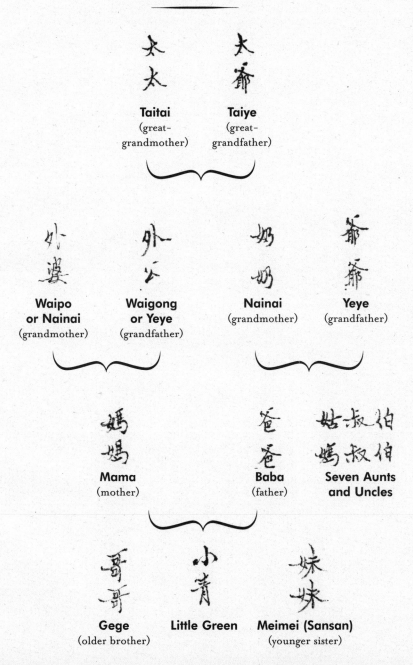

Taitai
(great-grandmother)

Taiye
(great-grandfather)

**Waipo
or Nainai**
(grandmother)

**Waigong
or Yeye**
(grandfather)

Nainai
(grandmother)

Yeye
(grandfather)

Mama
(mother)

Baba
(father)

**Seven Aunts
and Uncles**

Gege
(older brother)

Little Green

Meimei (Sansan)
(younger sister)

小青

I was born in a small city near the East Sea,
when the Great Cultural Revolution began.
My name is Xiao Qing, Little Green,
my country Zhong Guo, the Middle Kingdom.

When I was ten years old,
our leader died and the revolution ended.

And this is how I remember it.

Beginning

The year was 1966,
I was told,
five o'clock on a late spring afternoon.
Mama had been in labor for eight hours.
Baba was pacing up and down in the hall,
having just come from
a mass political meeting in the city square.

The doctor held me up in the air;
I was a ten-pound girl,
screaming loud with a little red face.
Outside the world was changing,
a revolution was in the making for my country.
Darkening clouds gathering in the sky above,
smothering thunders rolling on the horizon afar.
Mama sat on Baba's bike, holding me tight in her arms;
Baba peddled toward home against the cold night wind.
Mama's face was as pale as paper;
she caught cold on the way home,
during the weakest time after her labor.

Little Green

Little Green—Xiao Qing—
was the name they gave me.
Qing, the green
of tree leaves in early spring,
of clear water in a deep pond,
my baba said;
of beautiful youth,
the evergreen of life,
my mama said;
and of precious jade worn close to the heart,
my nainai said.

Mama's Name Has a Phoenix

Mama still says, telling me the story,
luckily for the illness,
she escaped the first struggle meeting
in the school where she taught
just by a day.

The beginning of
the Great Proletarian Cultural Revolution
was announced,
people waving red flags on the streets and
shouting loud the slogans on their red banners:
"Ten Thousand Years Chairman Mao!"
"Ten Thousand Years the Great Proletarian Cultural Revolution!"

Chairman Mao called to the country,
"Let's hold the large flags of
the Great Proletarian Cultural Revolution and
completely expose the reactionary position
of those so-called 'academic authorities.'"
The school where Mama taught was in the countryside,
but there was no escape even there.
It was declared to be "a revolutionary battlefield,"
like many other schools around the country.
The day before Mama went back,
in the school ceremony hall
the Red Guards stood on the stage,
the teachers were gathered around the stage,
and other students gathered around them.
The teachers picked
were denounced on the stage,
forced down on their knees and
beaten in front of the crowd.
They were asked to slap their own faces
while denouncing themselves aloud
until the Red Guards were satisfied.

Mama's name has a "phoenix."
The only child of our grandma and grandpa,
they called her Cheng-Feng,
which means "becoming a phoenix."
"You have no idea what trouble this could be,"
Mama told me.
"Phoenix is too traditional for the revolution."

Some said the old world needed to be destroyed
for the new world to come.
That's the idea of the revolution
I was born into.
That summer
around the country—our Middle Kingdom—
so many people died,
I was told many years later.

An Uncle Teacher Became a Counterrevolutionary

Spring 1967

"The Great Proletarian Cultural Revolution,"
Chairman Mao said,
"is a great revolution that will touch people's souls."

A year after the revolution started,
Liu Shao-Qi,
the other chairman of the country then,
besides Chairman Mao,
was "downed with" completely.
People used to call him respectfully
"Our comrade Liu Shao-Qi,"
but an uncle teacher used these words one day too late.

It was his turn to criticize
the denounced leader in a struggle meeting.

"Our comrade Liu Shao-Qi," he started with.
Just as he realized the mistake
and turned pale,
his head was already forced down.
"Down with the counterrevolutionary!"
people shouted,
throwing their arms up in the air,
trembling at this new discovery.
The uncle teacher slapped his own face,
calling himself one who "deserves to die."
He carried the label ever since I remembered.

A Dream

A dream was the first thing I ever remembered.
Mama was holding me in her arms,
snakes hanging from a big hollow tree,
wolves and hyenas running on the ground.

Mama was standing among these things,
holding me tight in her arms.

Go Up to the Mountains and Go Down to the Country

1968

I have a brother two years older,
who I called Gege.
Mama told me that
until the year I was two years old
and Gege was four,
the three of us had lived and traveled
between our home in the city where Baba worked
and the country school where Mama taught.
The city, like everywhere in the country,

had been deep in revolution.
The streets were filled with roaming Red Guards,
struggle meetings were held in every work unit,
and counterrevolutionaries were "downed with" every day.
A time of unpredictable changes,
a city of unrest.

Chairman Mao called to the whole country:
"Go up to the mountains and go down to the country,
to receive reeducation from poor and lower-middle-class peasants."
Baba was sent down from the city to labor
in a May Seventh Cadre School in the countryside.
We lost our home in the city.
My gege and I stayed with Mama
in the country school
after Baba was gone.

The Country Middle School

We lived in a long one-story house facing south
in the country middle school.
It had gray-blue tiles on the roof
with a brick wall of the same color.
Eleven other teachers' families
lived in the same building.
Eight of the families had children;
there were twelve of us altogether.

A river ran in front of the house.
Past the full-moon gate to the west of the house,
a brick bridge crossed the river.
On the other side of the river
was the school where Mama taught.

Between the house and the river was a long stretch of garden.
Right along the bank was the short bamboo bush
where wild red berries grew underneath.
Closer to the house were flowers mixed with vegetables:
daisy, tomato, and eggplant,
rose, pepper, and radish,
all between rows of cucumber frames.

Although Gege and I were too young to go to school,
our baba was sent away,
and our mama worked all the time,
we had many friends to play with.
We sometimes would sit in a circle and sing,
"Look, look, and look for a friend.
Find a good friend,
give a salute, shake a hand,
you are my good friend."
Our nannies,
young girls and grandmas from the nearby villages,
would be clapping hands, laughing and singing along

with their country accents.
The river was running and murmuring slowly by,
fish boats floating and wandering on the water,
red dragonflies dancing and gathering like dusk clouds.

Rice fields around our house turned
from green to golden yellow,
rose bushes along the river bloomed and withered,
months of spring and summer passed.
At these times, for us children,
the revolution seemed to be far away.

People Called Mama Beauty Lu

People called Mama Beauty Lu.
Lu is her last name
and she was a born beauty.
Her face had a smooth oval shape.
Her short black hair glowed under the sun.
Her skin had a light olive color.
Under her eyebrows like willow leaves,
her eyes were bright and clear as the sky.
In them I never saw a trace of fear or doubt.

When Night Fell

"The Great Proletarian Cultural Revolution
must be carried on to the end,"
Chairman Mao said, and
"The class struggle
shall never be forgotten."

After the political meetings and teaching during the day,
every night Mama had to go back to work.

The party wanted her to study
Mao's Little Red Book.

When night fell, all of the children were locked up at home.
To save energy,
no lights were left on for any of us.

Mama would get Gege and me to bed;
we heard her walking to the door,
pulling the string attached to the lightbulb;
then in darkness, we could hear
the sound of her putting the lock on the door.
It was too early to fall asleep,
so we would call to each other,
checking if the other was asleep.
Our friend Maomao was four years old
and lived right next door.
Being left alone all by herself,
she cried loud every night,
with such a bright voice,
angry, stubborn, and sad.
The whole building of locked-up children
listened to Maomao's cries night after night.

Sometimes in the middle of the night
I woke up to the sound
of Mama unlocking the door.
I heard her come inside,
sit down on a wooden bench in the kitchen,
and sigh alone in the quietness of the night.

A Parade in the Middle of the Night

One night, deep in our sleep,
we were startled by a loud cry outside.
"Get up, all the teachers and staff.

We just got a new indication
from the Party and Chairman Mao.
Get up, let's form a parade to celebrate.
Quick! Quick!"
There were footsteps outside the door,
and a flashlight shone through our window.
"Old heaven!"
Mama mumbled, getting up.
She scrambled to change to her day clothes.
I sat up on my bed,
dizzy, confused,
and still half dreaming.
"Mama," I cried,
and Gege called too.
"Go back to sleep.
It's not morning yet.
Mama will be back soon,"
she whispered.
We heard doors opening
and footsteps hurrying.
Mama rushed out but quickly rushed back.
She grabbed her Little Red Book
and hurried out again.
It sounded like a group had formed
in front of our house.
Someone started shouting slogans outside:
"Ten Thousand Years Chairman Mao.
Ten Thousand Years the Great Cultural Revolution!
Ten Thousand, Ten Thousand, and Ten Ten Thousand!"
And the rest of the people followed with sleepy voices.
Through our window
I could see shadows of hands
holding and waving the Little Red Books.
Maomao started crying next door again,
her voice louder and brighter than the slogan shouting.
"Wake up! Show your respect to our Party and Chairman Mao!"
the slogan leader taunted the parade group.

My heart trembled and I woke up completely,
hoping he was not yelling at my mama.
Then the group started marching toward west.
The shouting grew weaker as they marched away.
After a long time Mama came back, dragging her steps.
She shut the door behind her and said to herself,
"We all must be crazy!"

Mama told us later that
they had marched through the rice fields in the darkness
to the nearby town,
where there was a single street—
the only street around that they could march on,
and so it would be called a parade.
Their slogans echoed on the empty dark street,
where everyone was asleep and no lights were on.
They went back and forth on the same street for a whole hour.
Nobody came out to watch the "parade."
"People," each time Mama told the story
she would sigh and laugh, "all must be crazy then."

Uncle Xie and the Enemy Station

Uncle Xie lived three doors to our left.
He was a chemistry teacher sent down from Shanghai,
leaving his wife and three children behind.

He had a strange habit of
turning his radio on loud,
so loud that the whole building could hear it;
soon we no longer needed our own radio.
He left his door open whenever his radio was on,
even during the coldest winter days.
One day Mama and I were passing by and
Uncle Xie had his radio blasting toward the door
with an army song broadcasted:

"Forward, forward, forward!
Our army is facing toward the sun,
their feet stepping on our grand motherland!"
Mama said hello and asked curiously
why he always had the volume so high.
Uncle Xie smiled and said:
"If everyone listens to the radio with me,
who can say that I am listening to the enemy station?"

Some years later Mama told me that
Uncle Xie was born in a capitalist's family.
When he was young,
he studied in Japan as a chemical engineer
and came back to New China to serve his motherland,
but only to become the kind most suspected to be a spy.

Nainai Came to Take Care of Us

Spring 1969

My dear grandma,
my mama's mama, our waipo,
who we called Nainai,
came to take care of all of us.
So did many other grandparents.

My grandpa, our waigong, died a long time ago,
many years before I was born.
Nainai lived alone in the country,
close to her own baba and mama.
She was a petite little woman
who never stopped being busy.
Cooking, washing, sewing, and gardening
kept her busy all day long.

A Sphere of Light

Every day at six o'clock,
Mama came back to have dinner with us,
before she rushed back
to her political studies in her school.

At night things were quiet.
Nainai sat down under the dim yellow lamp,
sighing with great relief.
She liked smoking tobacco in a brass water pipe,
with water bubbling and
smoke surrounding her face.
Gege and I leaned next to her;
I loved the scent of tobacco and cooking on her clothes.

Often the electricity went out,
an oil lamp was all we had—
the light glowing only in a sphere—
beyond that, it was pure darkness.

I played the game of walking into the dark
with my eyes wide open.
At first I couldn't see anything;
my heart felt like it stopped beating for a second.
There was a temptation to turn back to the light.
But I stayed in the dark longer,
and the world started to take shape again.

Somewhere in the darkness, I thought,
Mama must be under another sphere of light
with Mao's Red Book in her hand.
Baba was too far away;
we couldn't imagine what his life was like
and whether he had a sphere of light too.

We Saw Baba Only Twice a Year

Chairman Mao said,
"All the bad things in the world
started from not laboring."

Baba lived in a May Seventh Cadre School,
where he was being reeducated.
The cadre school could only be reached by boat—
sometimes just a wooden boat,
slowly moved by a long bamboo stick.
It took a whole day each way.
We saw Baba only twice a year,
in the summertime
and Chinese New Year.
After not seeing him for a long time,
it felt so strange to call him "Baba" again.

The cadre school
was a big farm
with all sorts of grown-ups from the cities.
Intellectuals or people from wealthy families,
and also some people
who stood "on the wrong side" during the revolution.
Some of the grown-ups couldn't tell wheat from weed;
Chairman Mao thought it was good for them to know.
Those people were all sent to the country
to labor in the field and
to learn the life of the peasants
who were exploited in the "evil old society."

There was little I could remember about Baba.
When I was old enough to remember things,
he had already learned to work in the field.

To the Country

Spring 1969–1970

Nainai missed
her own baba, mama,
brothers, and sisters
who still lived in her village,
where the house and the fields needed
to be tended,
where she was a production team member
in the People's commune.

She brought Gege and me to the country to visit—
sometimes both or one of us at a time.
We lived in an old house
she and our waigong had built many years ago.
It became a home for us all.

The House

Like every old Chinese house,
Nainai's house faced south.
We lived in the west chamber,
where Nainai had her old red wooden wedding bed
with trees, flowers, and ancient beauties
carved on the red wood frame.

When springtime came,
the ground thawed,
softening, moistening underfoot.
We left the door open,
to the warm wind
and the swallows it brought from the south.
They made a nest on our long beam
and stayed for the whole spring,

busy carrying grass and worms in for their new babies,
who made little noises in the nest above our heads.

Taiye and Taitai

Nainai's baba, who we called Taiye,
and her mama, who we called Taitai,
lived close by
to the west in a small house
on a meandering creek
that connected to our pond.

The River, Riverbank, and Graveyard

Beyond the field behind our house
was a long riverbank
lined with Chinese scholar trees
heavy with white flowers in the spring and early summer.
Beyond the riverbank with the trees
was a river called the Ocean River,
running to the East Sea and the grand ocean far away.
Behind the riverbank and along the water
was a long long graveyard field
where everyone's ancestors were buried,
where Mama's baba, our waigong, was buried.
Snow white geese with red beaks,
crossing the green water in a long line,
hurdled idly by a farmer on a little boat with a small red flag.
Thin black dragonflies flew by,
gliding, and lingering ever so lightly
among the green grass and graves,
with wings like half-transparent black veils.
Ghost dragonflies,
the villagers called them.

The Lotus Pond

We had a pond to the west of our house.
Midsummer in the country,
lotus bloomed in the pond.
Pink, white, and rosy flowers
standing among round big green leaves,
waving and reflecting colors on the water,
like beauties wearing jade in the wind,
next to the humble water chestnuts
shyly presenting little moon-white flowers.
The pond was full of scent,
floating through the air far beyond.
A wooden bathtub moving in the water
was my little boat for the summer,
where I napped in the afternoon
and played with my friends,
under the lotus
and in the chorus of cicadas.

People's Commune

The system in the countryside was a People's commune.
Under each commune were the production teams.
One village was one production team.
Nainai was made a member of the team,
which she reported to every morning,
and where they assigned her work through the day.
She came back for morning, lunch, and afternoon breaks.
From the house I could see her working in the field,
bending over to weed the field,
stretching up to wipe off sweat.

Breakfast with Taiye and Taitai

Every house in the village had a loudspeaker
installed by the production team.
In the morning about five o'clock
the loudspeaker in Nainai's bedroom
would start to play "The East Is Red."

"The east is red,
the sun is rising.
A person named Mao Ze-Dong has been born in China,
he seeks happiness for the people,
he is the great savior of the people."

Then Nainai got up first
and cooked breakfast in the kitchen.
A little later she would wake me up
as the loudspeaker echoed through our home
broadcasting commune news:
"Under leadership of Chairman Mao and the Party,
the situation in the country is great!
So many and so many tons
of summer season rice
and cotton were produced,
it was double the expected production.
When production is good,
we do not forget about class struggle;
every production team is studying Marxism and
the thoughts of Chairman Mao."

Sometimes Nainai would ask me
to invite Taiye and Taitai for breakfast,
especially if it was a warmer day,
so they would not catch morning cold
on their way.
The morning air was so fresh,
I started running fast

on the small dirt road.
Endless rice fields beside the road,
changing color during seasons—
from tender to dark green in the summer,
from dark green to golden yellow in the autumn.
Brushing against sesame plants and long weeds,
with morning dew splashing all over,
soon I would be in front of their house,
calling Taiye and Taitai to come to the breakfast.
As I was running back ahead of them,
Taiye and Taitai followed behind me.
Taiye had a long white beard
that he often let me braid.
It waved in the morning breeze
next to Taitai's white hair.
The gray-blue smoke was thinning
from the chimney on Nainai's house.
We knew breakfast must be ready—
rice soup, steamed buns, and pickles,
and maybe also a few boiled eggs
with shells still hot
to warm my hands.

Taiye and Taitai would ask Nainai
about her day before and her day ahead;
Nainai answered describing work in the fields.
The loudspeaker of the radio would keep on talking,
but after a while we didn't hear it anymore.

Snowy Night

Winter 1969
Tian Lai

During the winter when I was four,
there were only Nainai and me

staying in the old house.
A few days before Chinese New Year,
we were looking at the moon one night.
It had a foggy ring around it,
like the smoke from Nainai's tobacco water pipe.
Nainai said thoughtfully,
"Spring fog, wild wind.
Winter fog, white snow.
White snow
promises a prosperous year."
We stood by the open door
as she spoke.
I smell the rich soil of the earth.

The next morning
the whole sky was covered
by a large cloud,
thick and heavy like a gray quilt.
By the time night was falling,
goose-feather snow was falling from the sky.

After dinner
Nainai said that
she wanted to see her younger brother,
who lived on the other side of our pond.
She put a pair of red-and-yellow tiger shoes on my feet
and a red silk cape with a hood on my shoulders.
She lit an oil lamp and put it in my hand,
then lifted me from a bench onto her back.
She blew out the oil lamp on the table,
closed the wood doors behind us,
and started walking toward the pond,
carrying me on her back.

The air was fresh, the snow still falling.
Winter fields under the snow
stretched endlessly into the night.

Nainai stopped walking for a second,
pausing to listen to something.
The lamp waved gently and stopped in my hand.
I heard, for a long second,
the snowflakes falling from the sky,
delicate, gentle: a little whisper
as each one passed by my ear,
landing ever so lightly
on my shoulder.

Perhaps
this was *Tian Lai,*
the sound from heaven
that old folks in the village spoke of.
"Only a lucky one would hear,
and perhaps, only once
in a whole lifetime,"
Nainai told me.

"Mengjiang Nu"

That winter I stayed with Nainai
for the New Year.
Mama took Gege to visit Baba.

Nainai had two sisters.
During every New Year
they came to visit their baba, mama, sister, and brothers.
Since our house had the most room,
they always stayed with us,
until the first full moon of the year.

Late in the winter, before the spring,
the fields were still frozen and quiet.
A few firecrackers went off here and there,
echoing in the crisp air near and far.

We went around to visit relatives and neighbors
every day for lunch and dinner.
The rest of the time we stayed at home,
gathered around lit bronze hand and foot warmers.
I had my own little hand warmer
where I roasted peanuts and broad beans.
When I heard the popping sound
and smelled the roasted scent,
I knew they were ready to be eaten.

Nainai sat by the table
with her sisters,
brewing a pot of hot tea.
Cracking sunflower seeds and eating small crispy fried dough,
they were sharing old stories they remembered.
They giggled with sparkling eyes,
as if they were young girls.
They talked about songs they knew,
songs I had never heard before.
Holding my hand warmer,
I sat among them.

The first time I heard Nainai sing,
she sang a song called "Mengjiang Nu,"
a story from two thousand years ago
about a young girl whose husband was sent far away from home
to build the Great Wall in the north for the emperor.
He died while she was on a journey to find him.
It went like this, beginning in January:

"In January the new spring,
every home lighting red lanterns,
husbands and wives reuniting,
Mengjiang Nu's husband building the Great Wall.

In February warm outside,
swallows come to the south.

All of them in pairs, in couples,
Mengjiang Nu is alone without her husband.

In March the Qing Ming festival,
every family visiting ancestors' graves,
Mengjiang Nu's family graves deserted.

In April busy caring for silk worms,
Mengjiang Nu collecting mulberry leaves
to feed the worms.
The basket hanging on the tree,
a handful of tears, a handful of leaves.

In May the beautiful sun,
every family busy in the field.
Others planting young rice seedlings,
Mengjiang Nu's field full of weeds.

In June so very hot,
mosquitoes and bugs flying and biting.
I'd rather have thousands of bloody bites on myself,
please spare my husband Wan Xiliang.

In July autumn wind cold,
every family sewing new clothes,
only Mengjiang Nu's clothes old and worn.

In August the wild goose door open,
frost under feet of single swallows,
Mengjiang Nu as sad as the single swallow,
love birds forced to separate.

In September daisies blooming yellow,
scent of daisy wine fills the vat.
Others' wine, couples drink together,
Mengjiang Nu is all alone.

In October north wind blowing,
reed catkins flying in the air.
The weather cold and bitter in the Great Wall,
how could Mengjiang Nu's husband survive at all?

In November the snow flowers blooming,
Mengjiang Nu reunited with her husband in a dream.
Walking thousands of miles to bring him winter clothes,
where is my love, my dear husband?

In December busy for the New Year,
every family sacrificing pigs and sheep,
Mengjiang Nu is watching her mourning room full of white."

Nainai's voice wandering in the air
up around the beam and down to my ears,
just like when she spoke—
not too high and not too low,
and not in a hurry at all.
Her sisters joined her here and there.
As she was singing,
Nainai was looking through the open wooden door,
into the field stretching far away.

I saw my nainai being Mengjiang Nu herself,
with her long black hair in a shiny long braid,
standing alone in the open field, looking far away,
waiting for my waigong to come back,
from whatever Great Wall and emperor he had left for.
Seasons changed around her year after year,
and she was still waiting there.

A Long Rest

1970

Just after the spring festival,
Taiye became very ill.
A bed was set up in his oldest son's home
in the large living room,
the center of everything.
The bed was set close to the floor
so he could move to the ground easily.
But he lay there quietly,
most of the time with his eyes shut,
as if he needed a long rest.

Nainai came whenever she had a break from the field,
helping Taitai to take care of Taiye.
She sat by him on a wooden bench,
with a bowl of porridge or soup in her hand.
She gave the food to Taiye by the spoonful.
He took a few spoonfuls each time,
then shook his head slowly from one side to the other.
She put the bowl down
and wiped his white beard carefully with a wet warm towel.

Summer came slowly that year.
Nainai's garden was full of green.
One afternoon
Nainai picked up a small watermelon,
and we went to see Taiye with the melon.
She cut the melon and said to me,
"Half for you and half for Taiye."
Then she gave me half the melon and a spoon.
I held it in my hand like a rice bowl,
and went to sit by Taiye.
"Taiye," I called.
He opened his eyes slowly,

as if waking up from a dream.
When he saw me sitting there,
a faint smile came to his face, as if from
somewhere far away.
I scooped the red melon,
and gave it to him.
He drank the juice and slowly chewed on the melon.
It was a hot late summer day
and the melon seemed to soothe him.

Nainai was sitting at the table
in the middle of the big empty room.
Taiye couldn't really see her from his bed,
but I saw her
wiping tears
from the corners of her eyes.

Autumn came,
and the days were getting cooler.
One afternoon I was in front of the house
playing with my friends.
Suddenly all the adults looked serious,
and they told us to stop running and not to make any noise.
Then I heard crying like singing from the house.
It was my taitai, the wife of Taiye,
and my nainai, the oldest daughter of Taiye.
Nainai was telling Taiye something:
"My dear father,
without you how do you expect us
to manage?
How tough your heart is,
to leave us like this.
Ever since I was a child,
you have been there for me."
Then I listened to Taitai and everyone else,
each of them singing their own stories.
I'd heard this kind of singing by women

in the country funerals,
where men usually cried silently.
Then I knew Taiye must have died.

In the country a funeral was called a white ceremony.
We had a white ceremony for Taiye that night.
They put him in a wooden coffin,
in the courtyard under the moonlight.
I went over to look at my taiye;
he was sleeping peacefully
with his white beard resting on his chest.
The neighbors all came over for the white ceremony banquet.
Each of them brought home a rice bowl for good luck.
The next morning they carried him,
crossing the golden wheat field of autumn behind our house,
and buried him under the Ocean River bank,
alongside my waigong.

A big sailboat with a tall white canvas sail
passed by soundlessly in front of my eyes.
I wondered if Waigong and Taiye were on the boat,
going somewhere else.
Perhaps they are going to the ocean,
where the river is running toward.
Perhaps they are going to cross the ocean,
where lies the unknown land.
Will I go there one day?
Will they all come to visit me on a big sailboat?

Little Sister Was Born

October 1970

After Taiye passed away,
Nainai and I returned to the country school
where Gege and Mama were.

Baba was still in the cadre school.
Mama told me a baby was coming,
her belly was like a small mountain.

Every morning before going to work,
Mama went to the river to wash our clothes.
Gege and I followed her.
When we came back,
Mama had a basket of washed clothes in one hand
and a bucket of water in the other.
"Aiya! You shouldn't carry heavy things,"
the neighbor aunties and uncles
cried as they saw her,
trying to carry the basket
and bucket for her.
But she walked fast,
shaking her head "no" and thanking them.

One morning, after we came back from the river,
Mama didn't go to work.
A midwife from the nearby town
rushed into our apartment with two other teacher aunties.
Gege and I were kept outside.
After a short while we heard a baby crying.
Our meimei—my little sister—was born.
When Gege and I were allowed back home,
the midwife and the two other aunties
were taking care of Mama in her room.
In the living room
Nainai was wrapping the baby in a red cloth.
She gently tied the cloth around her
and hooked the wrap onto an old steelyard
made of red wood and yellow bronze.
Moving the sliding weight carefully to balance,
"Six *jin*,"
she announced.
I smiled to myself,

knowing that I was still the biggest baby born to the family.
But my little sister was born the quickest.
"All that clothes washing and water carrying did it," Mama said.

Since the baby was the third child,
we called her Sansan, Little Three.
Baba could not come to see the new baby.
She cried often day and night.
"More than you and your gege ever did,"
Mama told me,
rocking Sansan gently back and forth in her arms.

On the Bridge to Mama's School

After Sansan was born,
for a while we all stayed together
in the country middle school—
except Baba, who was far away.
Nainai stayed home to take care of Sansan.
Mama was called back to school.

There were two political groups in Mama's school:
the "rebels" who wanted to
"down with" everything and
the "emperor protectors" who wanted to
"down with" only some things.
Mama didn't belong to either of them,
which made her life difficult.

The head of the rebellion group
was a young sports teacher.
Born into a family of three generations of peasants,
he proclaimed his roots were the most revolutionary of all.
Mama told me that
after the Cultural Revolution began,
instead of teaching, this man held struggle meetings,

calling teachers onto the stage and
deciding their fate according to his wishes.
He also organized a propaganda team.
With red bands on their arms
they performed "loyalty dances" to Chairman Mao every day.
They threw one arm up to Mao's picture;
with the other arm they held Mao's Little Red Book
pressed against their chests.
I couldn't help thinking that
the head of the rebellion group looked like a puppet,
not a man.

Like many teachers in the school,
my mama avoided him as much as she could.

One day after classes were over,
I was waiting for Mama on the bridge
while playing with my friends.
Mama came with some other teachers.
The rebellion group leader passed by Mama
and sneered her name,
which means "becoming a phoenix."
He said, "I guess your dead rich father was hoping
you would become a phoenix.
We received documents from your hometown.
Your background needs to be checked again;
there are suspicious things going on here.
Given the family you are from,
you could have counterrevolutionary motives."

My heart jumped to my throat.
I didn't understand what he was saying,
but I sensed that my mama was in trouble.

But Mama seemed to have been prepared for this.
She turned to face him.
"Comrade Li," she replied,

"I have been reading Chairman Mao's Red Book.
I am sure, being the rebellion group leader,
you study very hard too.
Could you point out on which page
our great leader said
the poorer you are, the more revolutionary you are?"

There was silence in the crowd.
Everyone was looking at him.
They knew that except for carrying and waving
the Red Book during slogan shouting,
this man had not read much at all.

Mama then continued calmly,
"If you cannot answer the question
about the Chairman's Red Book,
it's hard to say that you are more revolutionary
than the rest of us."

He flushed and yelled angrily,
"What is your attitude toward the revolution?"
No one had embarrassed him like this before.

Mama replied,
"I don't have any attitude.
But these people were once your teachers.
They have taught you how to read
and bought you books when you could not afford them.
If you have not lost your conscience,
think about what you have done to them.
Did Chairman Mao tell you to destroy their lives?
You are probably the one that is blackening the revolution."
His face now looked like
a purple pig liver on a butcher's bench.
"We will inform your husband's work unit;
you could be a counterrevolutionary couple together!"
Mama had fire in her eyes.

Before anyone had time to react,
she gave Li a big slap right on his face.
The two uncle teachers standing next to Li
quickly grabbed him by his arms,
reciting loudly a quotation from Chairman Mao,
"No armed struggle, only literal struggle!"
Li yelled and screamed like a wild dog.

So many admiring eyes around Mama,
she took my hand and said,
"Mama will explain things when you grow up."
Her eyes were as clear as the sky again.

I was scared for the things she was to explain,
and suddenly was afraid to grow up,
but my heart was soaring to the sky,
full of admiration for my mama.
We walked out of the crowd toward home
and never looked back.

Dance on the Toes: *The White-Haired Girl*

Winter 1971

There was a movie called *The White-Haired Girl,*
one of the "model plays"
developed by Chairman Mao's wife,
one of the only few movies allowed to be played.
It was about a peasant girl named Little Happy
who lived with her widowed baba.
The movie began on a New Year's Eve.
Little Happy's baba was hurrying home in a snowstorm,
dancing on the snow-covered road.

Little Happy opened the door for her baba.
She brushed the snowflakes from his shoulders,
as he presented her with a red hair string.
Jumping with joy,
she held the hair string between her hands,
dancing on her toes as she sang to her baba,
"Others' daughters have flowers to wear,
my father had no money to afford them,
he pulled two feet of red hair string
for me, Little Happy, to make my braid.
Ah, to make my braid."
All of a sudden the music grew dark and nervous.
A group of the landlord's "dog legs" rushed in,
led by the ugly young son of the landlord.
They asked for the field rent
that the old man couldn't afford.
They beat him to death in front of his daughter.
The villagers and a neighbor boy came,
and they fought the "dog legs" bravely,
but the young master pulled out a gun,
and they helplessly watched as Little Happy was snatched away.

She ran away from the landlord's house
to a cave in the mountains,
and her hair turned all white.
Finally her sweetheart, the neighbor boy,
who had joined the Communist Party's army,
came to the cave to save her.
The army liberated the village
and captured the landlord's family.
The White-Haired Girl, Little Happy,
danced on her toes and condemned
the evil of the landlord's family and the old society.
The neighbor boy,
a soldier now,
pulled out a gun.
The landlord and the young master were executed
while the villagers celebrated.

I was fascinated by the strange dance on the toes
and insisted that it would be
the only way I was going to stand.
Soon all of my shoes had open mouths on the toes.
Mama said that if I kept on doing this,
I wasn't going to have any more new shoes.
Nainai put patches on the shoes to cover my toes
as she and Mama laughed.
Gege and the other children laughed at my shoes too.

Gege was in second grade that year.
Every night he went to school
to practice in the school plays.
I followed him each night.
Watching him and other older children on the stage,
I danced on my toes,
hoping to grow up soon
to be in plays too.
The teacher in charge of the plays
was our neighbor.

She saw me dancing around
and asked my mama if I could
play the White-Haired Girl,
even though I was not in school yet.
Jumping on my toes, I yelled,
"Yes! Yes!"
By the end of the year, the special day came.
All the teachers, students, and their families
gathered in the school theater,
Mama and Nainai among them.
Gege was also performing that night.

I had never performed in front of such a big group of people.
When they announced the White-Haired Girl,
so nervous, I forgot the dance.
But with my arms up in the air,
I moved to the middle of the stage on my toes.
People started applauding and someone yelled "Good!"
I tried to dance,
and most of all, keep myself on my toes.
When the music reached its height for the final pose,
with great relief,
I kicked my leg high into the air and spun around,
and landed on the front of the stage
with my arms stretched forward to the future.

The light from above was blinding;
I couldn't see anywhere beyond the stage.
But I knew Mama and Nainai were somewhere there,
watching me from the crowd in the theater.
After what seemed like forever,
I heard the sound of applause and
got back to my toes.
With a smile I took a bow.

Gege's Revenge

The previous year Gege played a Chinese traitor
working for the Japanese army,
which he was not very proud of.
But this year he was a young heroic peasant boy
in a play called
The Rooster Crowing in the Middle of the Night.
His classmate who played the evil landlord
was a school bully
who once broke Gege's head with a brick.
I still remember the blood dripping from Gege's head
when Mama carried him, running to the school clinic.

On the stage,
in the middle of the night and behind a big tree,
the landlord pretended to be a rooster crowing at dawn,
"Ooh ooh ooh!"
All peasant workers were tricked to get up.
They labored in the landlord's field,
as the landlord waved a whip,
threatening and hitting them left and right.
This brutal exploiting went on for an hour.
At the end Gege came to the stage
with a big bag of grain on his shoulder.
Bending under the heavy weight,
he staggered all over as he walked.
Holding the whip and taunting loud,
the vicious landlord dashed onto the stage.
Gege threw the bag of grain on the ground
and gripped the landlord's collar.
The bag was stuffed with cotton and
bounced around but we all ignored it,
holding our breath, watching what was to happen.
Gege lifted his fist high up in the air and
gave the landlord, the school bully,
a big punch on his right cheek.

The landlord fell onto the ground,
his face full of surprise and confusion,
mumbling something in disbelief,
just the way it should be.
I knew Gege must have really hit him instead of pretending
and suspected the whole theater knew this too.
But then the audience cheered with excitement.
In the middle of the stage
Gege was trying to hide the smile of victory on his face
and look righteous as a young hero.
All the other peasants joined him,
waving their sickles and hoes in the air.
I jumped up and down on my toes,
so proud of my gege.

NAINAI'S STORIES AND OTHER STORIES

Nainai's Stories

Summer 1972

During summer vacation
Mama went with our little sister to see Baba.
Gege and I stayed with Nainai
at her house in the countryside.

At night,
under paulownia trees standing tall and straight,
we sat on a bamboo bed.
Stars glimmered in the sky above,
bugs and frogs sang in the rice fields,
scent of lotus floated in the night air.
"Nainai," I said,
"would you tell us a story tonight?"
Nainai waved her palm-leaf fan
and told us stories from a long long time ago.

"We once lived in a town by the East Sea.
A year before your mama was born,
terrible stories came from the south in the winter.
Hundreds of thousands in the city of Nanjing
were killed by the Japanese.
Streets, palaces, and city walls
were stained red by blood.
I was pregnant with your mama
when the Japanese came to our area,
killing people and burning houses along their way.
For almost eight years we were running and hiding—
not a day we lived in peace.
The Communist army came to fight the Japanese.
They were mostly guerrillas.
When they passed by at dusk,
they stayed in people's houses for the night.
There were both boys and girls;

the youngest I remembered
was only thirteen.
They loved to play with your mama,
laughing and jumping together like little children.
We cooked dinner for them
with the biggest wok we had.
The poor young things
moved around only by foot,
many miles each day.
We laid hay under blankets
on the living-room floor;
dozens of them slept side by side
with their weapons beside them.
They always moved out silently before dawn.

"Sometimes messengers from our army would come
to inform us that the Japanese might be coming.
The whole town would evacuate
to the reed marshes and fields that
stretched along the ocean.

"Once we were told that
the Japanese were coming from the west.
We kept watching the west for the sign,
until someone screamed,
'They are coming from the south!'
We all looked over to the south
about half a mile away;
the Japanese were coming to the town,
thousands of bayonets in the air,
reflection of the shining blades
blinding in the sun."

I felt afraid for Nainai, Mama, and Waigong.
Then I asked carefully,
"What happened then, Nainai?"

"Then we heard gunshots in the air,
busy like firecrackers on New Year's Eve.
Bullets suddenly were flying in the streets;
we all hid behind the kitchen stove.
Your mother's teacher, old Mr. Gu, lived next door,
to the west of our house.
When the shooting started,
his youngest son was in a store
on the other side of the street.
A bullet hit him as he ran to his family.
The older son tried to rescue the brother and
was shot on the street too.
Two sons killed in front of his eyes,
the old teacher went insane overnight,
his hair turned white within days."

"What about other neighbors?"

"Our neighbors to the east
were a widowed mother and her son.
The son was a hot-blooded man,
big and strong like a bull;
he fought the Japanese
in the Communist New Fourth Army.
The mother was sick at home for several years,
running and hiding from the war.
In the end she gave up.
The son came back home the day after she died,
crying and wailing through the whole night
like a little baby boy.
He buried his mother the next day,
wiped his tears, and went back to the army.
News came a few months later,
his head was hanging on a city wall
a hundred miles away from home.
The city was once the headquarters of the New Fourth Army,
lost to the Japanese in a big battle.

That city was where you were born.

"Now it is late,
Little Green.
It is enough for you to know.
And it's time for bed."

Lying in bed,
my eyes were wide open,
staring into the darkness,
where images from Nainai's story still vividly played.
"Go to sleep, Little Green,"
Nainai whispered,
and gently she waved her palm-leaf fan for me.
I closed my eyes
and slowly fell asleep next to her.

Candy Man

I was six when I was changing teeth;
I lost one of the top front ones first.
Nainai said,
"Toss it to the ground until you can't find it,
then it will grow down again."
Then I started losing the bottom ones too.
Nainai said,
"Toss it to the roof until it doesn't drop,
then it will grow up again."

One day, busy tossing my tooth toward the roof,
I heard somewhere
the sound of a flute coming near,
and children were yelling and running toward it.
"Malt candy!" they cried.
I stood up and looked to the road beyond our garden:
A man carried on his shoulder a wooden shoulder pole

with one basket on each side,
waving heavily as he walked.
He was blowing a small bamboo flute,
moving his head from side to side.
A group of children followed behind.
Running toward them, I forgot my tooth.

The man stopped one house down the road.
He opened the covers of the two big baskets,
our eyes all widening and sparkling in awe.
Each basket had a flat case on the top.
The one in the front had a big malt candy cake
with pieces cut so finely into small fan shapes.
The one in the back was full of small ribbons and hairpins
with shining bright colors
arranged so nicely next to one another.

The man took out a yellow brass gong
from underneath the front flat case.
He hit it once and announced:
"The size of the shoes will be the size of the candy!"
We squeezed around the baskets
looking at things we had dreamed of for months.
The loudest kids already brought shoes with them;
some others presented coins.
I pushed out of the crowd and ran to the house.
I went to the back of Nainai's bed,
found the pair of half-new leather shoes I had.
I squeezed to the side of the candy man.
He took over the shoes and looked at me with suspicion.
"You want to trade with these shoes?" he asked.
I bit my lips with my loose teeth and nodded my head.
Surrounded by envious eyes,
I got a piece of malt candy
big as the size of a shoe,
so heavy and chunky in my hand.

Then I saw Nainai coming toward us from the field.
She saw the candy in my hand and the shoes in the candy man's.
She reached to her pocket and took out
a few small bills wrapped with a handkerchief.
"How much?" she asked.
"One *yuan*."
Nainai hesitated; a couple of *yuan* was all she made
in a month working in the field.
"We will take half of the candy."
She gave him fifty cents and took back the shoes.

Nainai went back to the field and never spoke of
this again.

Walking on Thin Ice

Winter 1972

Winter had come to the country.
Ice was forming on rivers and ponds.
Nainai was still working in the field,
cleaning dried cotton plants off the ground.
I was running along the creek next to Taitai's house
and beating ice with a tree stick.
The ice, like dark glass
glimmering under the paling sun,
was tempting to step on.
As my friends watched,
I stepped on the ice and
moved to the middle little by little.
All of a sudden there was a cracking sound,
sharp and brittle, but unknown to my ears.
I was trying to make out the sound,
when the world suddenly vanished
as my body sank and
my head went under freezing water.

Kicking and grabbing, I stood up
in the water high to my neck,
so cold that everything hurt.
My friends were giggling first, then screaming,
"Help! Help! Little Green is in the water!"

Dragging myself through the water and ice,
I saw Nainai and Taitai running toward the creek,
Nainai in front, Taitai behind.
They both had bound feet.
One ran with more difficulty than the other,
one with hair grayer than the other,
both with frenzied looks on their faces.

They each grabbed one of my arms.
The next thing I knew we were in Taitai's house.
My teeth were chattering while everything else was numb,
and I could neither speak nor move.
After a long while I heard Nainai's voice.
"Little Green, come back home!"
she called, clapping her hands in the air,
around the house again and again
and then she went out to the small dirt road.
"Little Green, come back home!"
The sound of her voice and clapping of her hands
were going away and then coming back toward the house,
as if leading someone back from far away.
I gradually stopped shivering
and found myself tugged under a quilt.
Taitai was next to me,
holding a bowl of hot brown-sugar water.
"Little Green, come back!"
Nainai called again.
Warm tears slowly came to my eyes.
I heard them landing on the pillow
like raindrops from the sky.

"Life is like walking on thin ice."
In the years after,
my baba would say this many times to me.

Moving Back to the City on a Little Boat

Summer 1973

The summer when I was seven,
Gege and I were with Mama in the middle school,
while Sansan stayed in our old house
with Nainai in the country.
Our baba was still away from us.
One day Mama said,
"We are moving to the city where you were born.
Your baba might come back to the city.
We can be together that way."
I didn't know Baba very well.
It would be strange
to live with him.

We packed our belongings on a tiny wooden boat,
said good-byes to the families in the gray-blue tiled house
and our little friends.
They all followed us to the small dock down the river,
where Mama washed our clothes
and fetched water every day.
We got on the packed small boat, half sunk in the water.
The boat was rocking and so was my heart.
I couldn't stand up.
I had a feeling that this was not to be easy.

The farmer on the boat
pushed with a long bamboo stick.
The boat moved and we left the shore,
heading to the city twenty miles away.

The boat had a bamboo hut on it.
That was our room to spend the night.
Gege and I slept on a bench.
Mama sat on a little stool next to the door,
leaning against the wall and looking so tired.

In the middle of the night
I was thrown off the bench.
The boat was rocking like a cradle out of control,
with cold rain leaking nonstop from the roof.
Gege and I looked through the bamboo wall.
Under the flash of bright lightning
Mama was struggling to retie the boat to a tree.
The farmer was holding the boat with the bamboo stick,
which was about to break and fly into the wind.

I don't remember how,
but we got to the city harbor the next dusk
with all of our belongings drenched in the rainwater.

The storm
never
left my life.

CITY AND SCHOOL

City

The city was a strange place.
I didn't know anyone
and no one knew me.
Mama went around crazily,
trying to make a livable home for us.
Baba was not there to meet us,
but Mama said one day soon
he would come.

One afternoon
she left me alone on the city square to be picked up by her friend
while she ran to take care of things.
I waited and waited;
the sky turned dark.
I was tired and there was nowhere to sit.

A group of children came around.
They teased me and called me
a *xiang-xia-ren,* a country folk.
I didn't know then what to say.
Tears filled my eyes as I stood alone,
leaning against a platform taller than me,
with a big gray concrete statue of Chairman Mao
standing on top of it.
His feet were above my head on the platform,
his right arm stretched forward in the air,
pointing to the future somewhere.

Yeye and Nainai Southgate

Baba's baba and mama lived in a cotton processing factory
near the south gate of the old city wall.
To tell the difference from Mama's mama, the nainai we knew,
we called them Yeye and Nainai Southgate.
After the Party liberated the country,

Yeye was sent down here from another city
to be an engineer in the textile factory.

The Sunday after we arrived in the city,
Mama dressed up Gege and me:
me in my red cotton padded jacket with little flowers
that Nainai made and
Gege in his army-green Mao suit.
We each wore a Chairman Mao button on our jacket.
After we lost our home in the city when I was two,
we saw Yeye and Nainai only a couple of times.
Like many others in the city,
they were almost strangers to us too.

Mama told Gege and me,
"If people at the factory door ask you anything,
just say you are visiting your grandparents,
and don't say anything more than that."
Then we left, walking to the south.

We lived outside the north gate;
it was a long forty-minute walk to the south gate.
Gege was kicking the stones along the way.
Mama told him to stop.
"It took your nainai five nights to make these shoes.
Now you better quit kicking around,
and wait for your meimei before you run too fast."

The big gate to the factory was closed.
A young man with a red band on his arm
stopped us at the narrow side door.
He asked,
"Who in the factory are you visiting?"
Mama said Yeye's name.
"What is your relationship to him?"
"I am his daughter-in-law
and these are my children, his grandchildren."

"Which son are you married to?"
"The second," Mama answered.
The man pulled out a notebook and flipped to a page
with Yeye's name on the top
and a list of his children's names with notes for each.
He took his time to read the list,
then looked us up and down suspiciously.
I half hid my face behind Mama,
until he finally let us in.

The city had gates everywhere,
every gate had a guard with a red armband.
I always felt that I must have done something wrong.

First Lessons in the Elementary School

Fall 1973

I started school in the autumn.
After the class saluted the picture of Chairman Mao,
the teacher sat us down at our desks and stools.
Then we learned the following together,
"Ten Thousand Years Chairman Mao!
Ten Thousand Years the Great Proletarian Cultural
Revolution!"

We were also taught:
cabbage, radish, and one plus one is two;
singing, dancing,
and drawing pictures.

Baba Returns to Our Life

Winter 1973

One day in the cold winter
Baba came back to our life.
What a stranger he was to us.
Over the past five years
we had seen him only twice a year.

He wore a Mao suit in gray or blue,
the only two colors men wore in those years.
He was not very tall,
slim, gentle, and good-looking,
like a typical Chinese *du-shu-ren,* one who reads books.
He had large dark eyes with a tender kindness,
but there was something sad in his eyes.

He worked for
the urban construction department of the city.
Every day after he came back from work,
I saw him pacing in our small living room,
back and forth, back and forth,
as if trapped in something I could not see.

He tried to help Mama cook every night,
and was in charge of making rice.
After the pot started boiling,
he always forgot to turn the fire down.
We had burned rice many nights.

Gege and I complained to Mama.
Mama quieted both of us down.
She said to us in a low voice,
"Baba has a bother in his heart."

Squeeze Oil Beans

Winter 1974

During winter it was so cold,
and there was no heating.
As the north wind rattled and penetrated through the windows,
even with the cotton-cushioned shoes Nainai made for me,
the cold bit through to my toes like little icy snakes.
After sitting still in class for a while,
I couldn't feel if my toes were still there;
after another while I was losing my legs, too.
Then my mind started to drift.
How I missed my hand and foot warmers from the countryside,
and the beans and peanuts roasted in the warmers
while I drank hot tea with Nainai.

Then an electric bell rang loud for the end of class.
Some kids would call: "Squeeze oil beans!"
Hearing the words, we all ran to the door.
The air outside already filled
with excited screams of hundreds of children.
Rushing to the front of our classroom,
we quickly lined up with our backs against the wall
and our cheeks facing the sun.
Each one of us was an oil bean.
Splitting in the middle into two groups,
we started pushing and squeezing against one another.
Yelling and laughing as we squeezed,
other children's warm hair brushing on my face,
the icy little snakes finally left my toes.

Political Classes for an Eight-Year-Old

Spring 1974

I was eight years old.
They were teaching us Chairman Mao's revolutionary theory
in the political classes at school.
It said:
"In order to gain political power for the people,
we need to occupy the countryside first,
use the countryside to lay siege to the city,
and then seize the city."
Although required to memorize it,
I had no idea what this meant.
I imagined Nainai's house occupied by
uncle and auntie soldiers,
and then they would come to our house in the city.
When they stayed in our house in the city,
they would play with me.

I Love Beijing Tiananmen

Little Pretty was my best friend.
We were both eight.
Though Little Pretty was
too young to remember,
others had told her the
story of her growing up:
During the summer of 1966
the Cultural Revolution had just begun.
Words came from newspapers and radios
that Chairman Mao was on Tiananmen,
the Gate of Heavenly Peace,
inspecting millions of Red Guards
from all around the country
to encourage them to carry the revolution on.

Little Pretty's mama, a young teacher then,
went to join *Da Chuan Lian*,
a revolutionary mass rally,
a pilgrimage to our Great Leader.
She left on a late summer day,
when Little Pretty was a few months old.
Dressed in a grass-green army suit,
a red band on her arm, and
an army bag across her chest,
Little Pretty's mama walked toward the bus station.
She carried Little Pretty in one arm,
and held Mao's Red Book in the other hand,
while her husband chased her somewhere far behind.
At the north gate of the city
she left Little Pretty on the ground in the middle of the street.
Knowing her husband would pick up the baby,
she marched forward without turning her head back once.

Little Pretty's mama came back in the fall.
The green of her army suit faded,
but her cheeks bright and red,
and her beautiful phoenix eyes
on her fine long oval face sparkling,
she told stories everyone envied:
How she fought through the crowd
climbing shoulders and heads,
to get into the train through a window.
How everyone helped one another and shared food,
singing revolution songs all the way
with Chairman Mao in their hearts.
How in front of Tiananmen
she saw Chairman Mao on an open jeep
passing by far far away,
waving his hands to the ocean of youth.
Tears were running down everyone's face,
arms waving crazily to Chairman Mao.
Jumping up and down in the air,
some cried loud with mouths wide open,

some whispered to themselves in disbelief,
covering their mouths with trembling hands:
"Our Great Leader Chairman Mao!"

Little Pretty and I would walk to school together,
singing one of our favorite school songs:
"I Love Beijing Tiananmen,
above the Tiananmen,
the sun is rising.
Our Great Leader Chairman Mao
is directing us to march forward."

There Was a Time When Everything Was Rationed

Baba got sick after a while;
he was coughing day and night.
I thought,
It must be the bother in his heart
that Mama was talking about.
One day he went to the hospital and
they told him that he had a sickness in his lungs.

Mama said Baba needed nutrition to get better,
but everything was rationed during that time:
one and a half pounds of meat per family every month,
one egg and a small bottle of milk per family every week.
Early in the morning once in a while,
Mama made poached eggs in milk for Baba
before she hurried off to her school.
Baba took Gege and me by our hands and
led us to the kitchen in the back of the apartment.
On our small dining table
there were two small bowls of hot milk,
each with half a poached egg.
The milk was a little burned on the bottom of the pot,
but smelled really good.
The cut half eggs were soft and golden inside

and looked really delicious.
"Quick, eat it before it gets cold,"
he urged, and pushed us gently toward the table,
turning his head while coughing.
His thin back bent away from us
as he tried to regain his breath.

Something was swelling inside my chest,
my throat tight and nose sore.
I loved my dear baba;
he was no longer the stranger.
I wanted the bother in his heart to be gone.
I wanted him to laugh with us someday.

A Walk in the Park

Sometimes when Baba was out of his sad mood,
he carried Gege and me on his bike,
me in the front, Gege on the back,
riding to a park near our home.
We walked on the sand beach along the river.
Gege and I followed him,
picking up shells and splashing water onto each other,
laughing loud and running wild.

We walked until dusk settled in,
clouds above water burning red like fire.
It was time for us to go home.
Baba had a tender smile in his dark eyes,
but he never laughed with us.

Dinner

Seven o'clock every night
we all sat down at the dinner table.
First Mama and Baba would ask us about school and

Gege and I would tell our stories.

Then Mama would tell stories about her school,
which was always the best time of the day.
She would tell the trouble they tried to give her there and
how she reasoned and won the battle again.
Gege and I listened in awe,
our eyes lit with excitement.
Baba would be nodding his head here and there;
we knew he was proud of Mama too,
but he seldom told us about himself.

A Little Red Soldier

When I turned eight,
I was a Little Red Soldier
in the Young Pioneers group,
like almost everyone else in school.
Each of us had a little red scarf,
which we were told was
a corner of the five-star red flag of the country,
dyed red by the revolutionary martyrs' blood.
We wore our scarves to school every day.

The Jump Rope Song

Between school classes we had breaks.
We jumped rope and
played jumping the rubber band.

When we were jumping, we sang,
"Pomegranate flower is red and red,
I love our leader Chairman Mao.
Love study, love labor.
We are New China's good children."

Then the bell rang loud and
we rushed back to the class,
dragging ropes and rubber bands behind us in the dust.

War Games Against the "Foreign Devils"

During summer days
I followed Gege to play games with his friends,
mostly boys a couple of years older.
The wildest was the war game,
Chinese against the "foreign devils,"
the "good people" versus the "bad people."
Americans, Germans, or Japanese,
all the foreigners were devils against us.
I had only seen these devils in the movies about wars,
with guns and cannons killing people:
Japanese and Germans in World War II,
Americans in the Korean and Vietnam Wars.

We split into two different groups.
The leaders of the groups
did the rock, paper, and scissors game first,
and the losers got to be the foreign devils.
A line was drawn in the middle of the field,
which served as the border of our country.
"Chong-ah!"—"Rush!"
we screamed.
Both teams started rushing to the borderline,
waving sticks in our hands
until one side finally backed off.

Whenever I was on the good side,
the battle was often won.
I learned from the revolutionary heroines in the movies that
what you needed was a strong heroic attitude.
I would find the biggest tree branch around and

drag it behind me as I rushed forward,
staring at the foreign devils with my big dark eyes.
The boys halted their feet in front of me.
I heard them whispering to one another,
"This one is little but really tough!"
I was laughing so hard to myself that
if they had pushed me even a little,
I wouldn't have been able to stand.

Tomorrow's Soldiers

Every semester in school
we had a three-day army training
to prepare us to become soldiers tomorrow.

Early in the morning
many, many of us,
about a thousand,
were lined up in the school sports field.
We carried on our backs
quilts bundled tight into a tofu shape,
and in our hands
wooden spears decorated with red tassels.
Learned from uncle and auntie soldiers in the movies,
Gege and I also made camouflage hats
from leafy willow branches.
After instructions were given,
we started marching toward the school gate,
shouting, "One, one, one-two-one,"
stamping our feet like real soldiers in training.
Soon we crossed the south gate of the city
and marched into the country fields.
We sang army songs learned from school:
"The sky of the Liberated Area is bright,
the people of the Liberated Area are happy."
All of a sudden the march halted.

We heard a message being yelled down,
"Enemy planes discovered ahead!"
Hearing the message and remembering the rules,
we immediately threw ourselves to the ground,
yelling to one another, "Get down!"
Landing facedown and covered with dirt,
but still holding tight to my spear,
I twisted my head back and peeked through
the willow leaves on my camouflage hat,
imagining seeing in the sky
dark planes flying in large groups,
closer and closer, lower and lower,
just like in the movies I saw and
war nightmares I had,
dropping bombs like hail.

A Story About the Forest

Passed among children
were little-person books,
story books with persons drawn small on the pages:
"Dong, Chun-Rui,"
a People's Liberation Army soldier holding packs of explosives,
sacrificing himself while blowing up the enemy's block houses.
"Huang, Ji-Guang,"
another hero blocking the enemy's machine gun with his own chest.

We heard there were other kinds of children's books
confiscated and burned at the beginning
of the Cultural Revolution.
One time there was part of such a book
circulating among my friends.
The cover and most of the book were missing.
From the few worn pages that were left,
I read about a family who lived in the forest:

Baba and Gege had already left
for winter hunting in the mountains.
Mama was doing winter sewing.
A young girl was watching her baby brother
in a cradle next to a warm fire.
She pushed the cradle gently and sang a lullaby to him
that her nainai taught her before she passed away.

They waited for her baba and gege to come back,
bringing home winter quarries:
ring-necked pheasants with shining feathers,
brown rabbits with soft fur,
roe deer, fat with fragrant meat,
and maybe even a fire fox with a bright red color.
They waited also for the spring to come,
when the forest is covered by tender green leaves,
air glowing like a diamond under spring sun,
mushrooms coming out of the ground
like little umbrellas opening slowly,
which the girl will pick from the forest to be stewed
with wind-dried pheasant meat.

Growing up on a plain,
I never saw high mountains and forests in my life.
How fascinating this was and how it made me dream!

Suddenly, the baby stirred in the cradle.
The girl and her mama lifted their heads and listened.
They heard the crying of wolves
echoing in the snow-covered valley, and
sounds of the north wind.
The dark forest waved and surged like an ocean—

There the page was ripped in half,
a story with no beginning and no ending.
Which forest did they live in?
Will Baba and Gege come back and
will the family survive the winter?
I will never know.

Things to Learn

Summer 1974

Amidst all the playing in the summer,
Baba and Mama gave us things to learn,
things that were not normally taught at school.
One of the books we had was
Three Hundred Poems from the Tang Dynasty,
from which we recited one poem every day.

One was titled "Goose":

"Goose goose goose
Singing to the sky with a bending neck,
White feather floats on green water,
Red palms paddle in clear waves."

Another was "Spring Morning":

"During spring sleep
Morning arrived without notice.
Singing birds heard everywhere,
Sound of wind and rain came the night before.
How many flowers have fallen to the ground?"

We also practiced calligraphy,
which Baba and Mama had done
since they were children themselves.
Mama said,
"Your handwriting is your face when you write,
you don't want it to be dirty and ugly."
They taught us together
to sit up straight,
to suspend our wrists when holding the brush,
to grind the ink block to have the right concentration of ink,
to move the brush gently along the paper,
to apply strength when needed,
and to finish with confidence and determination.

Zhou Yu and Xiao Qiao

At night if we were not playing with our friends,
we sat on Baba and Mama's big bamboo bed.
Mama would be knitting a sweater for one of us.
Baba would have a book of ancient poems in his hand.
One night he was reading this poem
written nine hundred years ago about
a legendary couple from a thousand eight hundred years ago:

"The grand river, flowing to the east
waves, washing it all.
Extraordinary beings
last thousands of years.

To the west of the old fortress,
people said,
is the Red Cliff of Zhou Yu
from the years of Three Kingdoms."

He read it to us,
and said with a smile on his face,
as if seeing what he was describing:

"Zhou Yu was a young man,
handsome and the most talented in the country.
Xiao Qiao must have been sixteen or seventeen;
she knew books and poetry,
a beauty the whole country had fallen for.
One day on the grand river,
there were happy drumbeats in the spring air.
Yu, with all of his friends, waited with a banquet prepared,
his bride, Xiao Qiao, in a red silk wedding dress,
coming from another boat decorated with flowers and lanterns."
He paused and sighed with such feeling,
"What a beautiful time of life it must have been!"
Mama looked at him with a smile too.
She said before he continued,

"The children are too young to understand these things."
But I thought what he said was beautiful
and wanted to hear more.
Baba laughed a little at what Mama said,
looking at Gege and me apologetically,
and went back to reading his book again.
I imagined for the rest of the night,
the life he described in the poem,
and wondered by myself
where that time had gone.

Past Misery and Present Happiness

Every semester
the school invited peasants to our classrooms,
to tell us about their suffering in the old society.
It was a special class held in every school, called
Compare Past Misery with Present Happiness.
One year an old couple was invited
to tell the sad tale about a New Year's Eve
when they were young parents
with a baby and no home.

The husband started:
"It was after a drought year and
the field had produced nothing by autumn.
Unable to pay any rent,
right before the new year,
we were kicked out of our home by the evil landlord.
Hoping to go to our relatives for shelter,
we started for the city.
Carrying our baby, only a few months old then,
we walked in the midwinter cold for days,
begging along the way.
By New Year's Eve we still had twenty miles to go.
It started snowing as it was getting dark.

Holding the baby in her arms,
my wife couldn't move any farther.
I decided to walk around and beg for food.
My wife waited with the baby under a bridge."
The wife continued for her part:
"As my husband was looking for food,
I took snow from the frozen ground,
melted it in my mouth and fed it to the baby.
He was crying from hunger,
but gradually turned quiet with cold. . . ."

I remembered the snowy night in the countryside
when my nainai carried me on her back.
I had an oil lamp in my hand and
we had somewhere warm to go.
But on this snowy night in the same countryside,
the poor mother and baby
had nothing and nowhere to go.

I felt so sad for them, tears came to my eyes.
I knew if it was my dear nainai and me,
she would have also tried everything to save me.
I knew if they came to Nainai's door that night,
she would have given them food
and taken them in from the cold night.

As the story went on,
the classroom was at first in total silence.
Then the boy next to me started sobbing.
He put his face
on his folded arms on the desk.
Here and there my classmates were crying all around the room.

What injustice.
What unfairness.
And what evil society had caused such misery?
Our little hearts were filled with indignation
against the great injustices in the old society.

When I went home, Nainai was cooking in the kitchen.
The air was filled with the scent of stewed pork
and stir-fried vegetables.
I told her the story from school,
and asked her,
"Why were the landlords so bad?"
She didn't answer my question for a while;
instead she put a few pieces of pork
on a small dish for me to have before the meal.
She said,
"In the old time the poor did suffer a lot,
but some rich people were nice too,
helped poor people without asking anything back."
I was surprised by her answer.
From the stories told in school,
I couldn't picture a good rich person.
It would have been called
feudalistic backward thinking in school.
But I knew Nainai would not lie to me,
although I should not repeat what she had just said.

Baba Had a Dream in His Heart

After dinner during school days
we sat around the clean kitchen table,
Gege and I doing our homework,
Mama grading her students' work or exams
and preparing for the next day's classes.
Baba was often lost in his thoughts,
smoking a cigarette while sitting aside
and coughing hard in the half darkness.
Sometimes he stood up and
paced back and forth on the side.

Before the midterm or final exams
Mama helped us with arithmetic and reading.
Baba helped us with writing and politics.

In the political exams
one of the big things we were always tested on
was the advantages of the great Communism.
Baba was a Party member.
He would go over the list with us:
"First: In the great Communist system
people are equal to one another;
there is no difference between the rich and poor.
Second: In the great Communist system
everything will be shared by the whole society;
people work as much as they can,
but only take as much as they need.
Third: Right now we are developing socialism,
which is the prephase of Communism.
In the future not far away
Communism will finally be achieved in the world,
and the whole human species will be liberated."

Even to a child of my young age
the Communist world sounded fair and perfect.
With all the suffering in the old society
no one should ever want to go back.
Why should one have more than others?
Why should one be above the others?
"Wouldn't it be nice if all this came true?"
Baba was glowing under the light.
I never saw such delight on his face.
He continued,
"Perhaps such a thing would not be easy to achieve.
It would require suffering and sacrifice
from everyone in the society."

Baba had a dream in his heart.
I was touched by its light.

Mama listened without much comment,
but she did say a few times

that it would be nice if all this came true,
and she was certainly hoping so.

Qing Ming

Spring 1975

Early in the spring when
drizzle lasted for days,
there was a festival called *Qing Ming*,
which means "clear brightness."
Brown yellow grasses turned tender green,
long willow branches grew fuzzy little buds, and
seeds were newly sown in the field.
A time to *ta-qing*—to walk on the green—
a time also to remember dear ones who have passed away.
In an ancient Chinese poem
it says,

"By the time of *Qing Ming*
rain is frequent.
People on the road are
about to lose their souls."

When I was in the country with Nainai,
we would go to Waigong and Taiye's graves.
We laid out the dishes and rice liquor
we had carried over in a basket,
and lit a special kind of paper for the ghosts.
The fire glowed in the spring air.
Nainai held her cup with both hands.
She held it to the grave and took a sip.
"There,
take care of yourself
and keep the children safe in peace.
We miss you here day and night.

One day I shall come to be with you."
She gently extended the cup
up to the sky and down to the earth,
then to the ghost neighbors around.
"Please,
take care of him and he will take care of you.
He is a kind man, as you all know.
You neighbors, please,
help one another in difficult times
and keep one another company always.
I thank you here, before I come to your world."
She took another sip
and spread the liquor around on the ground.
Then I would get down on my knees
and touch my head to the ground three times.

After I started school in the city,
Qing Ming was celebrated differently.
"It's a time to remember the revolutionary martyrs
who died for our new China,"
the teacher said.
So we gathered early in the morning,
all lined up on campus.
We wore white shirts for memorial,
and red scarves around our necks as Little Red Soldiers.
Excited for the first spring outing,
we murmured and nudged one another in line,
until the teacher with a serious face
told us to stop and observe discipline.
We came to the People's Heroes monument in the city park,
with cement graves all around.

We sang a few revolutionary songs,
among them "The Quotation Song" from Chairman Mao:

"If we want to fight, there must be sacrifice,
death happens all the time,

but when we think of the interest and benefit of the people,
we die for a great cause. . . ."

We were told to stand in silent tribute for a whole three minutes.
After a minute I started to get nervous,
and felt that I couldn't hold my solemn expression any longer.
My face was going to break into a grin,
and I knew if anyone noticed,
they would make me a counterrevolutionary element.
I pulled my hair down around my face
and bowed my head deeply,
so nobody could really see me.
The tribute was finally over,
then stories were told about the heroes buried there.
Great details were given about their deaths—
how many gunshots they took,
how many enemies they killed even after they were injured.
I saw the images vividly in front of my eyes.
I also remembered the stories told by Nainai,
which made my heart feel heavy.
My blood boiled for their heroic acts:
How romantic it is to be a hero,
how happy one could be to die for what one believes in!

The ceremony was over and we were dismissed.
We played war games among the graves
and picked wildflowers in the new grass.
Usually I would get home early on these days.
Nainai would be sitting alone
in front of Waigong's picture in her room.
When dinnertime came,
we put a few dishes in front of the picture.
After the dinner Nainai took out the special paper
and we headed outside to burn it in the yard.
Mama chased us to the door.
"No, we can't do it here,"
she said anxiously.

"It's feudalistic superstitious activity, people would say.
We would be in trouble tomorrow."
Nainai sighed and stepped back inside.
She was sad the whole night and
became increasingly frustrated.
As she got frustrated,
she stamped her feet on the ground and said,
"They must be thinking we've forgotten them!"
I sat next to her and took her hands in mine.
"Nainai, I am sure Waigong and Taiye know,"
I said.

Learning from the Farmers

Every spring the whole school was sent
to the People's communes nearby
"to accept reeducation from the peasant class."

When I was in the second grade, we were told to weed a field
for the young cotton seedlings.
After some explanation by a few uncle farmers,
we all plunged into the field with great enthusiasm.
The fresh morning air had an exhilarating effect.
It felt great to be in the open country
where birds were singing
and wildflowers bloomed.

After some diligent plucking for an hour,
our attention wandered and
differences between seedlings and weeds became blurry.
The teacher had left a while ago
for a meeting at the commune headquarters.
When the sun was high and noon arrived,
a few commune members came back to the field.
The field was in a mess—
there were rows where cotton plants had been plucked

and weeds left untouched.
We were chasing, screaming, and running over the plants.
The farmers looked at one another in horror.
The oldest of them went away in a big hurry.
After a while he came back with our teacher.
I heard him talking as they walked toward the field:
"My good teacher,"
he pleaded,
"please tell the children to stop.
They don't have to work anymore for the day;
they can play for the afternoon and go home early.
We will take care of everything ourselves."
His tone was of such simple honesty and pleading,
the teacher was obviously touched,
and she felt so bad when she saw the field.
She apologized to the old man for the "help" we provided.
Then they came into the field to gather us.
"Good little children,
please do us a favor and stop.
Please step outside and play on the ridges."
He asked, but we went on
laughing and running around,
mimicking his country accent,
and calling one another "good little child."
His gentle bearded face was full of frustration,
half crying and half laughing,
as if he couldn't decide what to feel.
He stood in the middle of the field, helplessly shaking his head,
until the teacher finally gathered us together
and kept us in order.

We lined up to take lunch boxes from our school bags,
and walked over to the commune headquarters.
The auntie farmers had cooked us hot vegetable soup
in gigantic commune woks.
The front yard of the headquarters was
filled with a few hundred of us,

all chatting and eating like talkative finches,
excited to be in a big group.

When I got home that afternoon,
my cheeks were all red from the sun.
I told Baba and Mama the story of my day.
The same thing had happened to Gege's class.
We had a good laugh together.
Baba told us that in his cadre school
there was an old professor from Beijing
who wore thick glasses like the bottoms of glass bottles.
He was sent to watch over a small reservoir in the rice fields,
so that the production teams
wouldn't steal more water for their own fields.
After two days of watching the reservoir
the water level had dropped dramatically.
Only then did they discover that
he couldn't see a thing at night.
I didn't think our class would be asked back.
Neither did Baba think so.

Stinky Old Nines

To show that the traditional education system was wrong,
and that the intellectuals had so much to learn
from the working class,
some uneducated peasants and factory workers
were invited to the schools
to replace the teachers that
had been sent down to the country and streets
to be reeducated.
Classes taught by these replacement teachers
were in chaos.
Teachers like my mama and many parents watched with worry.

The Party had a system to classify social members.

Intellectuals, especially teachers,
were categorized as the number nine
type of despicable social members
among landlords, rich farmers, counterrevolutionaries,
bad elements, rightists, spies, and so on.
They were taunted as "Stinky Old Nines."
There were many "Stinky Old Nines" in our family,
including Mama and my big auntie
who taught in my elementary school.
We "stunk" quite badly through those years.

One time Mama's students got in trouble
with some factory workers who lived near the campus.
As Mama was trying to mediate between them,
a young factory worker shouted at Mama
in front of all her students,
"Don't try to teach us,
you Stinky Old Nine!"
But even after that,
both Baba and Mama
always insisted that we take our learning seriously.

A Mongolian Dance

I was on the school dance team,
where we were taught dances
with political themes.
Whenever there was a new movement
from the central government,
we went to the street to have a parade.
After some slogan shouting
the dance team performed on the stage in the city square.
I was leading the Mongolian dance.
During one part I jumped onto a chair,
started to bend my head and shoulders backward
while waving my shoulders gently back and forth.

I did this until my head was upside down,
almost touching my Mongolian boots.
I paused in that position for a few seconds.
The world was completely upside down,
a blur of red flags and banners,
Chairman Mao's giant head upside down too.
I started to make his face look straight,
imagining his mouth being his one eye
and his eyes connected into a new mouth,
then I started to do this to people
in the crowd surrounding him.
Suddenly feeling dizzy and almost falling off the bench,
I quickly lifted my head and shoulders back upright,
hearing remotely the cheering in the close crowd.
How strange the world can be
if only you turn your head upside down!
I thought.

Back in the Country

Summer 1975

During summers I often returned
to Nainai's house in the country.
For a few years
my little sister, Sansan,
stayed there with Nainai most of the year,
as Gege and I had done
before we went to school.
In the early summer when I was eight,
I went to the country to be with them.
Sansan was already four years old.
She had a round face and pink cheeks.

It started raining the day after I arrived.
Sansan and I stood by the north window
looking together into the rain.
The field was so green,
covered with a thin veil of light fog.
Beyond the field was the riverbank,
lined with Chinese scholar trees,
heavy with white flowers fully blooming,
swaying gently in the rain.
By the window with old wooden grids,
the air was sweet with the scent of flowers.
Sansan was gazing into the rain,
as if she was half dreaming.
She held on to my sleeves and murmured,
"Look, it's Waigong."
I followed her eyes carefully:
a yellow oil-painted canvas umbrella
was moving slowly under the scholar tree far away.
Underneath the umbrella,
someone in a long white mandarin gown—
like my waigong in the picture—
lingered along the long riverbank.

The Blue Ribbon

The next morning when Nainai was gone,
Sansan was going to show me some treasures
as she had promised me the day before.

We took a chair to the redwood cabinet
and stacked a little stool on the chair.
While I held on to the stool,
Sansan climbed up and
stood on tiptoes to reach the old bronze handle.
She opened the top door and
took out a shallow willow basket.

There lay a long blue ribbon of thin silk,
half a foot wide and several feet long,
half transparent,
with a color of the sky.
It had a hint of Chinese treasure blue,
the most beautiful color and texture I had ever seen.

I lifted it up in the air.
In the morning sunshine from the window
the silk was shining and glimmering,
like the wings of a blue dragonfly.
It flowed lightly and settled slowly down,
as if time and years were passing by in space,
as if purple flowers were waving in the field.
Sansan's eyes were sparkling.
I threw the ribbon into the air as high as I could.
We marveled together as it came back to earth.

We looked back into the willow basket.
Underneath where the ribbon had been,
lay a bracelet of a beautiful green stone
with the color of a deep pond.
It was broken in the middle.

"Must be jade,"
I whispered, and we nodded to each other,
as if someone would hear and disagree.
We pieced together the two half circles.
They fit so perfectly together along the broken edges.
But every time we let go,
the two pieces fell apart in a second.
We decided to put the bracelet together on the desk,
pretending it was never broken.
Then we returned to our blue ribbon,
carried it everywhere in and out of the house,
threw it again and again into the air as we jumped,
and stood still with our hands stretching out in the air,
waiting for something so delicate and beautiful to come back.

Nainai returned to the house from the field
while we were jumping in the bedroom
with the blue ribbon in the air.
She paused at the doorway and looked at us:
Everything seemed to move in slow motion,
the ribbon passing by our hands forgotten in the air,
dropping gracefully to the floor.
In these few seconds we remembered that
Nainai had never showed us these treasures.
We had taken them out without her permission.

She walked into the room and picked up the ribbon,
touched it gently with her rough palm.
A warm glow came to her face.
"Your waigong bought this for me from Hangzhou,"
she said.
"All silk dresses were burned
during 'Destroy the Four Olds.'
Only this small piece was left,
so light and hidden among the cotton cloths."
Then she picked up the broken bracelet from the desk.
A sadness overshadowed her eyes.

"Broken, cannot be pieced together anymore."
Sansan held my hand with hers.
We stood in the room in silence.
My heart filled with melancholy.

The next day we buried the bracelet
at Grandpa's grave,
covered with white flowers
fallen from the Chinese scholar tree.
Nainai gave us the blue ribbon;
it had become our own treasure.

Whispers at Night

Fall 1975

The summer was over.
Gege had stayed in the city with Mama and Baba.
I came back home,
leaving Nainai and Sansan in the country.
I missed them so much,
but I was also happy
to be with Baba, Mama, and Gege again.

One night,
after we finished homework,
Gege and I were sent to sleep.
Baba and Mama stayed up.
Somehow I couldn't fall asleep
and heard them whispering in the living room.
"The wind is changing direction again,"
Baba said, and he mentioned the name of a neighbor town,
then his voice lowered even more.
I vaguely heard that the movement in the town
was out of control.
Many had committed suicide and

corpses surfaced
in the river that ran through the town.

"Gege!"
I whispered to call my brother,
but he was asleep on his bed below.
I could only stare into the darkness around me.

"In my working unit
they are investigating my background again,
both about your father and my brother,"
I heard Baba continue.
Mama sighed heavily.
I felt more worried.
Then she continued,
"I can't change who my father was,
no matter what the Party thinks.
I know he was a kind and generous man,
and not everyone who had money was a bad person.
People who have a little common sense
should be able to tell the difference.
Something has gone wrong.
Some of the people who humiliated him before he died
were the people he helped the most.
Even the receipt of his contribution of land to the government
was used as evidence against him, that he had land and money."
There was a long silence.
"I guess you are right." Baba sighed.
"When my brother volunteered
for the Nationalist Party's youth group,
he was only thirteen
and had no idea what he was doing.
But now,
with these troubles in our families,
no matter how pure my belief is,
I won't have a future in anything I do."

Then they whispered a while more.
I couldn't sleep the whole night.
I wondered what had happened to Waigong,
how exactly he had died,
and couldn't help but think
what would happen to me if they asked me about him in school.

In the morning everything looked normal.
Baba was boiling hot water for us to wash our faces.
Mama was busy putting
boiled rice and a small dish of pickles on the table.
Their faces were peaceful as a still lake.
I thought to myself,
I must not let them or anyone know
that I heard anything last night.
Maybe it was just
a bad dream.

Big Liu

Early 1976

Big Liu was a teacher in Mama's school.
They called him a counterrevolutionary rightist.
When Big Liu was in college,
one of the party leaders fell in love with Big Liu's girlfriend,
and made Big Liu a counterrevolutionary rightist
to separate the couple.
Big Liu was sent to the countryside to be reeducated,
where he married another girl.
A few years ago he came back to the city to teach,
with his wife and two children,
a son and a daughter.
Other children called the two kids "small rightists."

Big Liu's old girlfriend went to teach

in another city in the south.
The grown-ups said she never forgot Big Liu.
In later years, after her husband died,
she found Big Liu again.
Big Liu went to visit her.
After he came back,
he shut himself in a room for three days
without drinking, eating, or talking.
With so many investigations going on,
there was little privacy in those years,
especially if you were a counterrevolutionary.
The whole school knew Big Liu's story.

It was during the winter break when I was nine,
one day right before New Year,
Big Liu's old girlfriend called the school gatehouse
and asked to speak to him.
There was a teacher-and-staff meeting going on.
My friends and I were
at the back of the meeting hall
as the adults talked about boring things.
The gatehouse guard came to the meeting and
found Big Liu in the crowd.
"Big Liu, there is a phone call for you from the south,"
he announced to the meeting.
"A woman," he added,
with a tricky smile on his face,
glancing and eyeing through the meeting hall.
People in the meeting looked at one another
and murmured in low voices.
There was no private phone during that time.
Big Liu got up as quickly as he could and
ran to the gatehouse to speak to her,
with the guard following right behind him.

During dusk we played outside.
A few kids chased Big Liu's two children,

while Big Liu and his wife fought at home.
"Your baba has a lover!
Your baba has a lover!"
Each time they chanted,
my heart twisted,
until a couple of teachers passing by
told them to leave the two children alone.
That was just the way life was.

Ten-Thousand-People Mass Meeting

Early Summer 1976

The city had a huge sports ground
where "ten-thousand-people mass meetings" were held
to announce new indications from the central government,
to summarize the victories of movements,
and also to sentence new counterrevolutionaries.
When the end of the meeting was announced,
the counterrevolutionaries were pushed
to an open prison truck,
and then forced to bow down to the crowd.
On the boards hanging from their necks,
a big red cross on each name
was followed by the words GUN DOWN IMMEDIATELY in red.
The truck headed to the execution field across the town.
The crowd stirred, thousands followed the truck,
joining hundreds already waiting on the street.
In the middle of the moving crowd like a thick circle of wall,
I felt so small and lost.
The next day a few boys showed off bullet shells
they had picked up from the execution field.

The third year I was in school, when I was ten,
I was chosen to be
the captain of the Young Pioneers group

and was asked to deliver a speech to
a ten-thousand-people mass meeting.

I put on my best white shirt,
a blue skirt from the school dance team,
and my red silk scarf.
It took two hours for the ten thousand people
to assemble on the sports ground.
A student fainted under the hot sun
and was carried away among murmurs of concern.
After an hour of speeches by grown-ups,
the mass meeting chairman called
the representative of the Young Pioneers to give the speech.
The open path to the podium
in the middle of ten thousand people
seemed to be infinitely long.
I walked and walked,
my heart pounding and my mouth dry.
I was afraid that I was going to faint too.
Finally I reached the stage.
My teacher lifted me onto a stool behind the rostrum,
then she squatted behind me, holding the stool.
I took out a piece of paper with my speech on it,
which my teacher had helped me to write.
I could hear the cracking sound of the paper,
amplified by the microphone and sent through the field.
"Dear leaders, teachers, and classmates," I started.
"Today we are happily gathered here to see that
under the leadership of our Great Party
and Great Leader Chairman Mao,
the situation around the country is all good!
We must study Marxism, Leninism,
and the thoughts of Mao Ze-Dong very seriously
and pass them down generation after generation,
so that the conspiracy of American Imperialism's
hegemony over the world
will never never succeed!"

Applause started around the field like spatters of rain,
as my pounding heart gradually settled down.

A Fight in the Field

Soon the semester ended
and summer break began.
I went with Gege to the country to be with Nainai.
Sansan stayed in the city with Baba and Mama.

One morning we heard a big noise outside the window.
Gege and I poked our heads out.
Two men were wrestling on the road by the field,
swearing and yelling at each other.
One was the leader of the production team,
the other a widower who lived on the south side of the village.
His wife had died suddenly the year before,
leaving three young children to be taken care of.
The villagers called him a *lanhan*—a lazy man.
His wife used to take care of everything for him.
Ever since she was gone,
he could barely keep his family together.
Food grains were distributed
by the production team every season.
He did nothing to plan for the long term and
squandered everything within days.
The rice vat emptied as soon as it was filled.

Underneath the *lanhan*'s feet
were scattered ears of wheat and a cotton bag.
The leader of the production team was taunting the man:
"You thief, stealing the state's grain!"
Around them were a few production team members.
Some were laughing, but some were shaking their heads.
A couple of older ones were trying to separate the two.
The field had been newly harvested the night before.

The widower must have come back
to pick what was left in the field.
Nainai came up to the window and looked at the fight,
sighed heavily, and stamped her foot on the ground.
"It hurts the conscience to starve these children!"
Gege turned his head around and asked Nainai,
"Nainai, so who is good and who is bad?"
Nainai hesitated for a moment and she said,
"Both are not good!"
But Gege was certainly not satisfied with her answer.
He tugged on Nainai through the whole day,
"Come on, Nainai, there must be one of them that is right!"

At dusk we picked tomatoes from our garden,
packed them with a few steamed buns in a basket,
and headed to the south of the village.
The sky was darkening into a deep blue;
the wind was big;
trees by the road swayed heavily,
like large dark shadows against the sky.
We passed by the widower's house
where he and his three children lived.
The house was dark.
They had probably run out of oil for the lamp.
Without calling into the house,
we laid the food in front of the doorsill,
and left quietly in the darkening night.

Gege and I were each at Nainai's side that night,
before I fell asleep, I heard Gege mumbling while yawning,
"Nainai, so who is the good person
and who is the bad person?"

Nainai told the story for many years.
"One must be good and one must be bad!
You tell me which one is which!"
she laughed every time.
She never answered Gege's question.

Cut the Tail

Early in the morning a few days later,
the loudspeaker in the house
announced an order from above
"to cut the tails of capitalism,"
which Gege and I thought was funny.
We chased each other around in the front yard,
threatening to cut each other's capitalism tail off.
Then the loudspeaker called for an emergency meeting
at the production team headquarters.
Nainai left the house in a hurry.
She came back from the meeting at noon.
She said that according to the proclamation,
the private family plots,
which would be the garden in our front yard,
would be confiscated as the "tail of capitalism."
The plants would all be pulled out of the ground the next day.

After a whole spring and early summer
of planting and watering,
the tomatoes were just starting to ripen under the green leaves.
Some melon flowers were still blooming on the fence.
The biggest melons had just grown to the size of my little fists.
The sunflowers along the roadside
were only a couple of feet tall,
with tender yellow flowers following the sun around.
Nainai sighed.
"It hurts the conscience to destroy these crops.
What crime did the plants commit?"

We had a quiet dinner that night
and went into the garden with Nainai,
each with a basket in hand.
Bright moonlight like flowing water
fell from the sky above us
and coated the garden and plants in silver.

We picked a few tomatoes that were ripe
and cucumbers that still had the tiny pricks on them.
I secretly worried about my lotus in the pond
where the flowers had just started to bloom
and some new leaves were still coming out of the water.
Would that be the "tail of capitalism" too?
I dared not to ask.

Then we sat by the garden as we usually did
on a warm summer night.
I asked Nainai to tell a story.
She sighed.
"A difficult time is not easy to pass."
Then she told the war stories again.
"The house was looted so many times,"
she said.
"Each time when we returned after the Japanese came,
all the cabinets and cases were wide open.
Left on the floor were things they couldn't carry
but could destroy.
Clothes and quilts all torn apart,
rice and flour scattered all over.
Sometimes we ran away while cooking a meal.
When they arrived, they were too afraid to eat the food.
They'd poked holes all over the wok with their bayonets.
We were still lucky compared to the other town,
where streets of houses were burned to ashes.

"After the Japanese,
local thugs organized the 'landlords' restitution corps.'
They knew even better where and whom to loot.
One year I brought your mama
back here to visit my family.
Your waigong was staying at home alone.
One night someone knocked on the door.
He called your waigong's name a few times
and asked,

'Can I borrow your fire for a smoke?'
Your waigong was a warmhearted person,
willing to help even strangers,
let alone someone who spoke the local dialect
and knew his name.
He opened the door and there was a group of them
with their faces covered.
They pushed into the living room,
tied your waigong up in a chair,
and started searching the house.
Your waigong struggled out of the rope
as they were busy looting.
He grabbed a gong behind the door and
rushed onto the street, hitting it loudly.
Some neighbors came out of their houses and
the looters ran out through the back door."

Ah, there must have been no place safe in this world
but the reed fields along the ocean, I thought.
I saw my mama as a little girl with big clear eyes,
Waigong holding her in his arms,
Nainai standing next to them among the tall reeds,
looking at black smoke rising high
to a sky red from burning fire,
without knowing if it was their home or the neighbor's.

The next day a group of young production team members
came to each house in a frenzy.
All the families stood in front of their houses
and watched the cutting of "capitalism's tail."
Tomatoes and melon vines were pulled out of the ground,
left to wither in the hot sun.
All the sunflowers had their heads chopped off.
Then the "cutting team" went to the pond,
yanked my lotus out of the water,
and moved on to the next house.

A Big Earthquake

July 28, 1976

Another emergency meeting was summoned
suddenly one day.
A big earthquake had happened before dawn
in a northern city called Tangshan.
So many died and many still buried under the rubble,
the number in the hundreds of thousands.
"We have come to a time of frequent earthquakes,"
the government announced.
In the areas prone to earthquakes
all were ordered to live in tents.
At dusk Baba arrived from the city,
as we struggled to build a tent in front of the house.

We went home with Baba to the city the next day.
The whole city was moving out,
building tents on every piece of open space.
For the weeks after,
people who had gone to the disaster area to help
came back with terrifying tales:
"The sky first flashed with eerie blue lights,
then the earth started shaking violently,
burying tens of thousands of families under fallen roofs.
The sky then glowed red for days
from fire burning all over the city."
Old people who were superstitious whispered,
"Heaven and earth are angry,
the dynasty will change soon."

Chairman Mao Died

September 9, 1976

It was a hot September day;
I was home taking a nap in the tent,
drifting in and out of patches of dreams.
There was a weird voice circling in the air.
"It can't be worse!
Chairman Mao is dead!"
I rushed out of the tent half awake,
thinking I was still in my dreams.
Then I saw a fat woman who was our neighbor
walking between houses and tents
while flapping her arms in the air.
With a high-pitched voice she repeated,
"Chairman Mao's dead!"

My head was spinning
and I thought to myself:
It can't be possible.
It can't be true.
What happened to
"Ten Thousand Years Chairman Mao"
and
"Ten Thousand Years the Great Cultural Revolution?"

A Big Mourning Hall

The whole country became a big mourning hall;
wherever there were people, there was crying.
We were summoned back to school
immediately after Chairman Mao died.
There were no classes.
Teachers were crying, students were crying.
This went on for days.

Sometimes it was unclear to me what I was crying for.
I had only seen Chairman Mao's pictures and statues,
but I guess it was supposed to be sad
that he didn't live for ten thousand years,
and people who knew him
would never be able to see him again.
Then I thought of my nainai and taitai:
Imagine if this dying happened to one of them.
I would never see them again,
just like I never saw my taiye again after he died.
Life is strange. I have no control over it!
The thoughts made me very sad,
and I cried for a long long time after that.
But then I ran out of reasons to cry again,
while some others were still crying.
I started to worry,
wondering if they had deeper feelings
for Chairman Mao than I did.

Walking on the City Wall

This city used to have a city wall;
endless battles happened around it.
The attackers came from the outside of the wall,
the defenders fought back from the top of the wall.
Old folks recalled bloody times,
in loud shouts of "kill,"
knives shining and flying in the air,
heads and arms chopped off,
falling to the ground under the city wall.

This was the road I walked to school and home every day.
The city-guarding river still flowed by the side,
yellow wild daisies blooming in the autumn sun,
bees humming in the flowers.
I was wearing a black band on my arm

and a white paper flower in my hair for Chairman Mao.
Kicking dirt under the yellow daisies,
I saw a couple of bones scattered along the water.

Holding the bones in my hands,
I sang my jump rope song under the fading dusk sun,
"Pomegranate flower is red and red,
I love our leader Chairman Mao. . . ."
I climbed back to the top of the fallen wall,
walking to
home at the other end.

EPILOGUE

IN THE EARLY SUMMER OF 1966 a revolution called the Great Proletarian Cultural Revolution started in the People's Republic of China. During that summer the revolution swept through the vast land of 9.6 million square kilometers of China. In the name of the revolution and led by young students, armed fighting, beating, smashing, and looting spread over the country. Thousands of people were beaten to death that summer, among which, many were teachers killed by their own students. In the same year, from August to November, from the Gate of Heavenly Peace of the Forbidden City, Chairman Mao inspected thirteen million revolutionary youths from all over the country and encouraged them to carry the revolution forward. In 1968 Mao called to the country for a reeducation movement. Millions of intellectuals, students, and government cadres were sent down to the countryside to labor in the fields and receive reeducation by peasants. The revolution continued for ten years—until Mao's death in 1976. During those ten years, tens of millions—from highest-ranked government officials to common people—were denounced and persecuted as counterrevolutionaries, rightists, spies, landlords, and bad elements. Millions perished. Now the era is referred to as the "Ten Years of Great Calamity," by the people as well as the government of China.

I was born the moment the Cultural Revolution began. As a child, I grew up half blind to and half aware of the glory and cruelty of such a revolution. It took me many years to learn some of the facts but perhaps never the total truth of an event that brought a nation such suffering. Through my own memories and stories I heard from my family, I want to give you this story, in hope that life is not wasted and the world will not live through the same suffering again and again. And above all, the will to live shall always be trusted.

GLOSSARY

Armed struggle *(Wu Dou)*: A denouncement with physical attacks.

Baba: Father.

Counterrevolutionary: A person who performs a political activity in opposition to an earlier revolution or who is against a revolution.

Destroy the Four Olds *(Po Si Jiu)*: A search of homes to confiscate and destroy anything that is traditionally of rich class, including fine arts, clothes, furniture, and books of no revolutionary content.

Dog leg *(Gou Tui Zi)*: A person who works for someone with power.

Down with *(Da Dao)*: To denounce, criticize, and overthrow.

Gege: Older brother.

The Great Networking *(Da Chuan Lian)*: In August 1966 the Red Guards around China began a period of revolutionary networking *(Chuan Lian)*. Millions of Red Guards flooded Beijing by train and bus, some even on foot. From August to November 1966, Mao inspected thirteen million Red Guards at Tiananmen Square and encouraged them to carry on the Cultural Revolution.

Jin: A Chinese weight unit. One jin equals 1.1 pounds, or 0.5 kilogram.

Literal struggle *(Wen Dou)*: Denouncement by criticizing verbally.

Little Red Book *(Xiao Hong Ben)*: A small book of Mao's quotations with a red cover. During the Cultural Revolution people were encouraged to carry copies of the Little Red Book whenever they could and wherever they were. The quotations became the standard by which all revolutionary efforts and even daily life were judged.

Liu, Shao-Qi: Born in 1898. In 1959 Liu replaced Mao as state chairman and was considered to be the successor to Mao until the Cultural Revolution began. In 1966 Liu became one of the major targets of struggle during the Cultural Revolution. In October 1968, Liu was officially denounced and expelled from all of his positions. He died in a prison in 1969.

Mama: Mother.

Mao, Ze-Dong/Chairman Mao: Born in 1893. In 1931 Mao became the chairman of the Chinese Soviet Republic. In 1949 he proclaimed the Chinese People's Republic and became the Chairman of China. In 1959 Mao was replaced by Liu, Shao-Qi as the state chairman but retained his chairmanship of the Party politburo. In 1966 Mao launched the Cultural Revolution and reasserted his leadership. In 1976 Mao died at age 83.

May Seventh Cadre School *(Wu Qi Gan Xiao)*: Farms set up in 1968 in accordance with Mao's directive released on May 7, 1966. In the directive Mao suggested setting up farms where cadres and intellectuals would be "sent down" from the cities to labor in the fields and receive ideological reeducation.

Meimei: Younger sister.

Model plays *(Yang Ban Xi)*: During the early to mid 1960s Mao's third wife, Jiang Qing, developed "eight model plays" in the format of Chinese opera and western ballet, all with contemporary and revolutionary themes. These model plays were made into movies. During the Cultural Revolution these movies were the only ones watched around the country, and the plays were the only performances seen in theaters.

Nainai: Grandmother.

Qing Ming: "Clear brightness"; Chinese memorial day festival.

Red Guards *(Hong Wei Bing)*: At the beginning of the Cultural Revolution a group of middle and high school students in Beijing named themselves "Chairman Mao's Red Guards" and followed Mao's call to "rebel against the system." Mao's support of these students encouraged the name "Red Guard" to be adopted by groups of young people, mostly in their teens, all over China. Vowing to protect Chairman Mao and his revolutionary line, the Red Guards ruthlessly attacked "bourgeois" intellectuals, "bureaucrats," and "capitalist roaders," and some eventually turned against each other with armed fights, resulting in the loss of lives and great destruction of the society.

Rightist *(You Pai)*: During the Anti-Rightist Movement, from 1957 to the early 1960s, tens of thousands of people were labeled as rightist. Most of the accused were intellectuals. Some of them were sent to "reeducation through labor," some were imprisoned, and some were executed.

Stinky Old Nines *(Chou Lao Jiu)*: In the Cultural Revolution intellectuals were ranked ninth on the list of class enemies—which also included landlords, rich farmers, counterrevolutionaries, bad elements, and rightists.

Struggle meeting *(Pi Dou Hui)*: A meeting held to denounce and criticize people, during which the denounced were humiliated and often physically attacked.

Taitai: Great-grandmother.

Taiye: Great-grandfather.

Waipo: Grandmother—mother's side only.

Waigong: Grandfather—mother's side only.

Yeye: Grandfather.

Yuan: A Chinese monetary unit. One yuan equals about one eighth of a dollar.

Acknowledgments

I would like to thank my editor, Paula Wiseman, for recognizing this book at an openhearted first glance and for her guidance along the way; my fabulous book designer, Mark Siegel, for introducing the book to Simon & Schuster and everything he did for the book; and Susan Midlarsky, my once fellow writer from the MIT Writers' Group, for introducing the book to Mark. If not for you all, this would not have happened.

I would like to thank my agency, the Sandra Dijkstra Agency, for their kind support and guidance for a first-time author, particularly Jill Marsal and Sandra Dijkstra.

I would like to thank Robin Lippincott, my writing teacher at Harvard Extension, for his gentle guidance; Hans Guggenheim, Baird Brightman, and Winston Jones for their belief in the book since the moment I met each of them; and Maxine Hong Kingston for her inspiration as a writer and as a human being.

I would like to thank all my friends in the U.S., China, and Europe for their love and support; those who were the first readers of the book while I wrote it in Cambridge, Massachusetts—Kathryn, Daisy, Susan, and Tim—and my writers' group in Marin, California—Leslie, Rosemary, Kirk, and Sara—for their comments and encouragement; and Merche, Jeff, Xingchen, Marta, Ginny, and many others for being there during happy and difficult times.

Mostly I would like to thank my family in China: my mama, baba, nainai (who passed away six years ago), gege, and meimei (Sansan), who have given me so much in my life, including this book.

About the Author

Chun Yu was born in China and grew up there. After graduating from Peking University, she moved to the United States to pursue her Ph.D. and a career in science. She now works as a principal scientist in a medical company. Chun Yu lives in San Rafael, California.